MOLORA

Yaël Farber

MOLORA

Based on the *Oresteia* by Aeschylus

OBERON BOOKS
LONDON

WWW.OBERONBOOKS.COM

First published in 2008 by Oberon Books Ltd
521 Caledonian Road, London N7 9RH
Tel: +44 (0) 20 7607 3637 / Fax: +44 (0) 20 7607 3629
e-mail: info@oberonbooks.com
www.oberonbooks.com

Reprinted in 2010, 2011, 2012 (twice), 2015

Visit www.oberonbooks.com to read more about all our books and to buy them. You will also find features, author interviews and news of any author events, and you can sign up for e-newsletters so that you're always first to hear about our new releases.

Contents

Foreword

by Yaël Farber, Director and Adaptor

'This thing called reconciliation... If I am understanding it correctly...if it means this perpetrator, this man who has killed my son, if it means he becomes human again, this man, so that I, so that all of us, get our humanity back...then I agree, then I support it all.'

Cynthia Ngwenyu, mother of one of the murdered Gugulethu 7, when facing her son's state-sanctioned murderer at the TRC

In the aftermath of South Africa's transition into democracy in 1994, the world held its collective breath in anticipation of a civil war that would surely unleash the rage of generations shattered by the Apartheid regime. South Africa defied expectations, however, lighting the way forward for all nations trapped in quagmires of revenge. Despite the praise Nelson Mandela received from 'First World' leaders for heralding great restraint through this transition in our troubled land, nothing could convince those same leaders to check their own ancient eye-for-an-eye, knee-jerk response and their resulting offensives of 'Shock and Awe' on the women and children of Baghdad. South Africa's relatively peaceful transformation was an extraordinary exception in our vengeful world

But such a journey is neither simple nor easy, and has little to do with the reductive notions of a miraculously forgiving Rainbow Nation or 'turning the other cheek'. In the epic eye of South Africa's storm, it was not the gods – nor any *deus ex machina* – that delivered us from ourselves. It was the common everyman and everywoman who, in the years following democracy, gathered in modest halls across the country to face their perpetrators across a table, and find a way forward for us all.

The ancient *Oresteia* trilogy tells the story of the rightful heirs to the House of Atreus, dispossessed of their inheritance. Forced to live as a servant in the halls of her own father's house, Elektra waits for her brother Orestes to return from exile to the land of his ancestors and take back what is rightfully theirs. The premise of this ancient story was striking to me as a powerful canvas on which to explore the history of dispossession, violence and human-rights violations in the country I grew up in. I had long been interested in creating a work that explores the journey back from the dark heart of unspeakable trauma and pain – and the choices facing those shattered by the past.

Molora is an examination of the spirals of violence begat by vengeance, and the breaking of such cycles by the ordinary man.

In the long nights following the devastating attack on the World Trade Centre, amid the grief, recriminations and the Bush administration's indiscriminate wielding of revenge, a fine white powdery substance gently floated down upon heart-broken New York.

Our story begins with a handful of cremated remains that Orestes delivers to his mother's door...

From the ruins of Hiroshima, Baghdad, Palestine, Northern Ireland, Rwanda, Bosnia, the concentration camps of Europe and modern-day Manhattan – to the remains around the fire after the storytelling is done...

Molora (the Sesotho word for 'ash') is the truth we must all return to, regardless of what faith, race or clan we hail from.

The Power of Speech

by Sophie Nield

In *Molora*, Yaël Farber's version of the *Oresteia*, a character – a human person – is subjected to torture. The method used is called the 'wet-bag' technique: the person is handcuffed and a wet bag is applied to their face so that they begin to suffocate. The use of this technique was revealed in 1995 by security policeman Jeffrey Benzien, in testimony given to the Truth and Reconciliation Commission in South Africa.

The wet-bag technique produces suffocation but it also prevents speech. The person, deprived of breath, is unable to testify to their experiences and is denied not just the right to speak but the right to be heard.

The work of South African director Yaël Farber is deeply concerned with these questions. She has written and spoken of her profound belief in speaking as a form of healing. 'Speaking and being heard is a modest but profound beginning,' she has said. 'The shattered history of South Africa will take generations to heal but I believe theatre has a significant role in this process.'

Molora engages with speech on many levels: speaking for ourselves, speaking to others in theatre and speaking to and for each other before the law.

It is based on Aeschylus' ancient Greek trilogy, the *Oresteia*, which is about the famed curse on the House of Atreus. The events of the trilogy represent a family, and a state, driven apart by violence and revenge. King Agamemnon, returning from the Trojan War, is murdered by his wife Klytemnestra. Their daughter Elektra conspires with her long-lost brother Orestes to kill their mother in revenge for Agamemnon's death. Orestes, having slain his mother, is then pursued by the Furies, ancient spirits of vengeance and retribution.

In resolution of these conflicts, the Goddess Athena brings together twelve jurors to hear the case and decide on the verdict. Apollo speaks for Orestes; the Furies, avengers of the crimes of patricide and matricide, speak for the dead Klytemnestra. In the end, the verdict is split equally and Athena legislates for mercy and reconciliation. The play marks a transition from the law of retribution

– an eye for an eye and a tooth for a tooth – to the administration of justice by a jury representing citizens – based in speaking, witnessing and hearing.

'I have long wanted to create a work that explores the cycle of violence and the dilemma of survivors who have to choose between the impulse to avenge and the impulse to forgive,' Farber has commented. *Molora* imagines the *agon*, or formal debate, between Klytemnestra and Elektra, which is heard by the Chorus, composed of Xhosa tribeswomen from The Ngqoko Cultural Group.

The argument takes place in the context of the Truth and Reconciliation Commission (TRC), convened in Cape Town in 1995 to deal with the aftermath of Apartheid.

During the three-year process of the open public hearings, three committees heard evidence from all sides: perpetrators, victims, security forces and resistance groups. The TRC was empowered to make recommendations for amnesty and reparation to the State President, for crimes that were deemed demonstrably politically motivated and proportionate, and where there was full disclosure. This process was not without controversy but the principle was that in speaking and being heard, reconciliation and forgiveness – healing – becomes possible. Restitution, not retribution.

The TRC based itself on a constitutional commitment to '*ubuntu*', a Bantu word meaning a philosophy of being human. The Chair of the TRC, Archbishop Desmond Tutu, has described it thus:

> '**A person with *ubuntu* is open and available to others, affirming of others, does not feel threatened that others are able and good, for he or she has a proper self-assurance that comes from knowing that he or she belongs in a greater whole and is diminished when others are humiliated or diminished, when others are tortured or oppressed.'**

Farber has noted that 'the power of having a listener was evident during the TRC…to own the events of one's life and share these memories is to reclaim one's self and offer your community, your witnesses, a collective possibility to do the same'.

The Italian writer Adriana Cavarero has written about narrative and selfhood: about what happens when we hear our own story from the outside, told by another – how through hearing and being heard, we learn who we are. Here, as in Farber's creative process, the life is not the story – the shape of the story comes afterwards. Cavarero writes on the examples of Oedipus, who learns who he is when he hears his terrible history, and of Ulysses, who learns the significance of his life when he hears it sung. Meanwhile, the French philosopher Maurice Merleau-Ponty once wrote, 'the spoken word is a gesture and its meaning a world'. By speaking, or speaking out, we manifest the possibilities of justice and of community: of standing for, and standing up for, each other.

The theatre represents the world to us. Dramatic characters, especially tragic characters, may function as metaphors for the epic scale of suffering and cycles of narrative – but they also remind us of how the epic scale is, in the end, about being human. This is perhaps *ubuntu* again: in the Zulu phrase, 'a person is a person through other persons'. In this way, the characters stand in for and speak for us all.

In Aeschylus' *Oresteia*, the Furies are the avengers of patricides. This word is linked to the father, but also to the land, and thus can perhaps imply not only murder of the father but also of the land. In South Africa's reconstruction of itself through the mechanism of the TRC, fury and revenge gives way to reconciliation. The world is remade. As Farber has commented, 'the barriers we construct to differentiate ourselves from one another collapse under the weight of the evidence when we all inevitably share these fragile "once-upon-a-times"'. We can find reconciliation in the theatre.

Sophie Nield is Head of the Centre for Excellence in Training for Theatre at the Central School of Speech and Drama, University of London. She writes on questions of theatre, space and representation in political life and the law, and on nineteenth-century magic shows.

The Ngqoko Cultural Group

The Chorus Reinvented

The Ngqoko Cultural Group is a body of men and women committed to the indigenous music, songs and traditions of the rural Xhosa communities. Hailing from the humble rural town of Lady Frere in South Africa, the group was first formed in 1980. A single bow player and her daughter were maintaining the practice of playing music together, when a German visitor, Dawie Dargie, began working with the Xhosa musicians with the help of Tsolwana Mpayipheli as translator. In 1983 Mpayipheli, or 'Teacher' as he is respectfully known, discovered several other musicians who joined the group. They have since established a reputation as guardians of the rural Xhosa culture, maintaining the survival and presence of indigenous South African music and instruments.

In *Molora* the device of the ancient Greek Chorus is radically reinvented in the form of a deeply traditional, rural Xhosa aesthetic. Farber chose to collaborate with The Ngqoko Cultural Group with the intention of rediscovering the original power of the device of the Chorus in ancient Greek theatre. In her quest to find a group that could represent the weight and conscience of the community – as she believes is the Chorus' purpose – she happened upon the unearthly sound of the Ngqoko Group's UMNGQOKOLO (Split-Tone Singing).

Farber drove out to the rural Transkei to meet with the women, where she told them the story of the *Oresteia*. The reaction to the story was deeply felt and met with much discussion on the moral implication of killing your own mother. Farber instantly knew she had found the Chorus to this new *Oresteia*.

Trained in this ancient art of singing, these women have been taught from an early age, the skill of creating this vocal phenomenon, as well as being masters of the ancient musical instruments that are an intrinsic part of their everyday lives in the rural Transkei. The mouth bows, calabash bows, mouth harps and milking drums form an array of traditional musical instruments that they – as Chorus – play in accompaniment to the text of *Molora*. The sounds of these unique

Xhosa artists lend a haunting texture of sound, which is unfamiliar to most modern ears, and evokes a deeply emotional accompaniment to the work.

The envisaging of the Chorus as a group of 'ordinary' African women provides the context of the Truth Commission, which witnessed thousands of such 'ordinary' folk gathering in halls across South Africa to hear the details of a loved one's death at the hands of the State.

The individuals that constitute The Ngqoko Cultural Group represent, in this context, the unique grace and dignity that was evident in the common man who chose a different path for South Africa. Within the Ngqoko group are two spiritual diviners who are trained in the channelling of ancestral powers. While these women are restrained in their use of authentic trance on stage, their authority in spiritual conduct allows a moment in which the audience may experience a deep participation in a prayer to our ancestors for an end to the cycle of violence in South Africa – and indeed the world.

Acknowledgements

- **Yana Sakelaris** for her dramaturgical contributions and assistance when adapting the text

- **The Ngqoko Cultural Group** for their songs, praises and traditional practices which profoundly shaped this work

- **Bongeka Mongwana** for her Xhosa Translations

- Past and current cast members, with whom *Molora* grew and continues to grow

- This work was first made possible by **Standard Bank National Festival of the Arts**

MOLORA

Dedicated to Lindiwe Chibi, *Molora*'s original Elektra

Your light continues to shine for us all

A Note on the Quotations

The patchwork of quotations from the original Greek plays used in *Molora* are flagged up in the footnotes: where the translations are known they are identified with initials (see below); where I have been unable to rediscover the original version I quoted from, the references are followed by (SU), ie 'source unknown'. The known sources are:

Aeschylus, *Agamemnon*
> LM: Louis MacNeice (Faber, 1967)
> RF: Robert Fagles (Penguin, 1977)

Aeschylus, *The Libation Bearers* (*Choephoroi*)
> IJ: Ian Johnston (http://www.mala.bc.ca/~Johnstoi/aeschylus/ libationbearers.htm) [line numbers refer to the translation]

Sophocles, *Electra*
> RCJ: Richard Claverhouse Jebb
> (http://classics.mit.edu/Sophocles/electra.html)
> DG: David Grene, from Grene and Lattimore, eds, *The Complete Greek Tragedies* (University of Chicago Press, 1957)

Euripides, *Electra*
> ECP: Edward Paley Coleridge
> (http://classics.mit.edu/Euripides/electra_eur.html)

The line numbers of the Greek text are given in square brackets at the end of the footnotes. These are taken from the following Loeb Classical Library parallel editions of the relevant texts: *Aeschylus*, vol II (William Heinemann, 1957); *Sophocles*, vol II (William Heinemann, 1961); *Euripides*, vol III (Harvard University Press, 1998).

Characters

KLYTEMNESTRA

ELEKTRA

ORESTES

CHORUS OF WOMEN
&
TRANSLATOR

The first British performance of *Molora* was at the Barbican Centre on 9 April 2008, in a production by the Farber Foundry in association with Oxford Playhouse (originally produced in association with The Market Theatre, Johannesburg). The cast was as follows:

KLYTEMNESTRA, Dorothy Ann Gould

ELEKTRA, Jabulile Tshabalala

ORESTES, Sandile Matsheni

CHORUS & MUSICIANS, The Ngqoko Cultural Group: Nofenishala Mvotyo, Nogcinile Yekani, Nokhaya Mvotyo, Nopasile Mvotyo, Nosomething Ntese, Tandiwe Lungisa, Tsolwana B Mpayipheli

Creator and Director Yaël Farber

Assistant Director and Dramaturgical Contributor Yana Sakelaris

Vernacular Text Translators Current and past cast members

Instrument and Song Arrangements The Ngqoko Cultural Group

Set Designers Larry Leroux and Leigh Colombick

Costume Designers Natalie Lundon and Johny Mathole

Lighting Supervisor Paul Peyton Moffitt

mise en scène

This work should never be played on a raised stage behind a proscenium arch, but on the floor to a raked audience. If being presented in a traditional theatre, the audience should be seated on stage with the action, preferably with all drapes and theatre curtains stripped from the stage and the audience in front of, left and right of the performance. Contact with the audience must be immediate and dynamic, with the audience complicit – experiencing the story as witnesses or participants in the room, rather than as voyeurs excluded from yet looking in on the world of the story.

The ideal venue is a bare hall or room – much like the drab, simple venues in which most of the testimonies were heard during the course of South Africa's Truth and Reconciliation Commission: Two large, old tables – each with a chair – face one another on opposite ends of the playing space. Beneath Klytemnestra's testimony table is a large bundle wrapped in black plastic. Upon each table is a microphone on a stand. Between these two tables is a low platform which demarcates the area in which the past / memory will be re-enacted. Centre of this platform is a grave filled with the red sand of Africa. Beside it lies an old pickaxe. Neither the grave nor murder weapon can be seen when the audience enters – as the platform is initially covered with a large industrial sheet of black plastic.

Along the back of the playing area, upstage and facing the audience, are seven empty, austere-looking chairs, upon which the **CHORUS** of **WOMEN** – who will come to hear the testimonies – will sit. The audience is seated in front of and around the performance area, as if incorporated into the testimonies. They are the community that provides the context to this event. Seated amongst audience members are the seven **CHORUS** members, as well as **KLYTEMNESTRA** and **ELEKTRA**.

prologue

*As the audience wait for the play to begin, an elderly Xhosa
woman emerges from the audience, and moves in silence
into the performance area. She is dressed with the modesty
characteristic of rural women from the Transkei. She has clay
on her face and a blanket about her shoulders. She walks over
the platform and considers the space. Holding a corner of the
plastic sheet which covers the platform – she gently begins to
gather it towards her. In the silence, the plastic drags away to
reveal a richly-toned, earthen floor. The performance space,
now fully visible, has a bleak beauty. In the centre of this
earthen floor is the grave. The woman seats herself beside the
mound of red soil, picks up her traditional calabash bow and
begins the ancient singular sound of the UHADI (Calabash
Bow). She sings softly in Xhosa:*

Ho laphalal'igazi.

[BLOOD HAS BEEN SPILT HERE.]

*One by one, the other **WOMEN** of the **CHORUS** rise gently
from the audience, and move towards the stage, joining
the song. All are dressed simply, with blankets around their
shoulders. The last member of the **CHORUS** is a man in a
hat and old suit. They take their places on the chairs upstage
and continue singing. **KLYTEMNESTRA** – a white woman
in middle age – rises from the audience, crosses the playing
space and takes her place at one of the wooden tables. She is
here to testify. **ELEKTRA** – a young, black woman – follows,
and sits at the opposite table. Perpetrator and victim face one
another at last. The **CHORUS** concludes its song. in silence,
the UHADI (Calabash Bow) is passed quietly down the line
of **CHORUS** members, and laid on the ground. The silence*

*ensues – lasting almost a minute. Everyone waits without emotion or movement. Finally, **KLYTEMNESTRA** pulls the live microphone towards her. An ominous sound fills the room, as it scrapes along the wooden table. The neon lights above the tables and **CHORUS** flicker on. The Hearings have begun.*

i: testimony

KLYTEMNESTRA: [1]A great ox –
As they say –
Stands on my tongue.

As she begins to speak – the CHORUS all turn their heads to the right, to listen to her.

TRANSLATOR: Ndise ndayinkukhw' isikw'umlomo.
[A GREAT OX...
AS THEY SAY...
STANDS ON MY TONGUE.]

KLYTEMNESTRA: [2]The house itself, if it took voice, could
tell the case most clearly. But I will only
speak to those who know.
For the others – I remember nothing.

She pauses before her testimony. It is hard for her to speak.

[3]Here I stand and here I struck
and here my work is done.
I did it all. I don't deny it.
No.
He had no way to flee or fight his
destiny –
our never-ending, all-embracing net.
I cast it wide.

---

1   The Watchman in *Agamemnon* (LM), p 14 [36]

2   The Watchman in *Agamemnon* (LM), p 14 [36]

3   Adapted from Clytemnestra in *Agamemnon* (RF), ll 1398–1415, p 161 [1379–1392]

I coil him round and round in the robes
of doom... And then I strike him once,
twice, and at each stroke he cries in
agony.
He buckles at the knees and crashes here!
And when he's down I add the third –
the final blow,
to the god who saves the dead beneath
the ground.
I send that blow home...
in homage...
like a prayer.
So he goes down, and the life is bursting
out of him - great sprays of blood.
And the murderous shower wounds me,
dyes me black.
And I... I revel like the Earth
when the spring rains come down.
The blessed gifts of God.
And the new green spear splits the sheath
and rips to birth in glory!
[4]Here lies Agamemnon my husband
made a corpse by this right hand.
A Masterpiece of Justice.
Done is done.

TRANSLATOR: Kugqityiwe.
[DONE IS DONE.]

---

4   *Agamemnon* (RF), ll 1429–31, p 162 [1395–6]

ELEKTRA – who has been listening silently – draws the live microphone towards her. We hear it scrape slowly along the rough table top.

ELEKTRA: Ndingasiqala ngaphi isicengcelezo sam ngenkohlakalo yakho?
[5][WITH WHICH OF YOUR EVILS SHALL I BEGIN MY RECITAL?]
Kona, ndingayeka phi na?
[WITH WHICH SHALL I END IT?]
Zange ndayeka ukuyilungiselela into endandiya kuyithetha ebusweni bakho…
[I HAVE NEVER CEASED TO REHEARSE WHAT I WOULD TELL YOU TO YOUR FACE…]
If ever I were freed from my old terrors. And now I am. So I pay you back with these words I could not utter before: You were my ruin…
Kodwa ndingakwenzanga nto.
[YET I HAD DONE NOTHING TO YOU.]
You poisoned me with your deeds. You are the shadow that fell on my life and made a child of me through fear. I have hated you so long…
And now you want to look into my heart? You who did this to my father will pay. [6]For if the dead lie in dust and nothingness,
while the guilty pay not with blood for blood –

_____

5   Adapted from *Electra* (Euripides: EPC) [907–8]

6   Adapted from *Electra* (Sophocles: RCJ) [245–6]

Then we are nothing but history without
a future.

*The CHORUS breaks into UMNGQOKOLO (Split-Tone
Singing – the powerful, ancient form of 'throat singing'
that traditional Xhosa women train in from an early age).
KLYTEMNESTRA and ELEKTRA slowly rise from their
chairs, maintaining eye contact. They move out from behind
the safety of their tables and square up on the periphery, at
opposite ends of the raised earthen floor.
In a decisive moment, they step onto the earthen floor. With
this gesture, mother and daughter commit to the process
of unearthing the past. ELEKTRA pulls her dress down to
expose her back and shoulders. KLYTEMNESTRA receives
a pot of hot water and cloth from one of the WOMEN of the
CHORUS.*

ii: murder

*ELEKTRA is a child of seven years. Her mother washes her
with the steaming water from the pot. ELEKTRA sings softly
to herself, over the sound of the UMNGQOKOLO (Split-Tone
Singing) which will continue throughout the following scene:*

ELEKTRA: (*Singing.*)

One man went to plough
Went to plough the mielies
One man went to plough
Went to plough the mielies
Two men went to plough…

KLYTEMNESTRA wraps ELEKTRA in a blanket, embraces her as though in farewell, and then rises with determination. She grabs the end of the pickaxe that lies on the ground. She drags it behind her, in a trance. It scrapes audibly along the wooden platform. She heads towards her testimony table.

ELEKTRA: Mama…uyaphi?
                            [MAMA…..WHERE ARE YOU GOING?]
                            Mama…mama…?
                            Uyaphi Mama? [WHERE MAMA?]

KLYTEMNESTRA climbs onto the table with the axe raised high above her head. She screams, and slams the axe onto the table. With this blow, she has struck her husband – Agamemnon – dead. She squats on the table and, scooping from an enamel bowl, covers her expressionless face, arms and hands in blood. She jumps from the table, and pulls at the plastic bundle hidden there. The body of Agamemnon – played by the actor who will perform the part of ORESTES – is revealed. ELEKTRA screams.

ELEKTRA: Mama yintoni le uyenzileyo?
                            [MAMA WHAT HAVE YOU DONE?]
                            (*Running to her father's body and flinging
                            herself onto it.*) Tata uyandibona na?
                            Uyandibona Tata?
                            [DADDY CAN YOU SEE ME? CAN YOU SEE ME
                            DADDY?]

KLYTEMNESTRA pulls her daughter off her dead husband. ELEKTRA fights her way back to the body several times. KLYTEMNESTRA throws her from it brutally.

KLYTEMNESTRA: Don't look!

*The **CHORUS** concludes their **UMNGQOKOLO** (Split-Tone Singing).*
*In the silence we hear **KLYTEMNESTRA** panting with effort. She drags the body towards the grave and begins to bury him in the soil. A **WOMAN** of the **CHORUS** plays **ISITOLO-TOLO** (Jew's Harp) as the actor rolls away and rises slowly, leaving **KLYTEMNESTRA** to finish covering where she has concealed the corpse. He recedes and exits, dragging behind him the black plastic he was wrapped in, and a trail of dust in the air. **ELEKTRA** grasps the other end of this plastic as though to hold him earthbound, but is forced to release him as he disappears. **KLYTEMNESTRA** moves to the pot of water and methodically begins to wash the blood from her arms, hands and face. **ELEKTRA** crawls to her father's grave.*

ELEKTRA: (*Screaming in grief.*) PAPAAAAA!!!!

KLYTEMNESTRA: [7]Here I stand...
                        And here I struck...
                        And here my work is done!

*She throws the bloodied cloth into the pot of water, with force. The water spills over the sides of the Pot. The **CHORUS** sings in **UMNGQOKOLO** (Split-Tone Singing).*

---

7   *Agamemnon* (RF), ll 1396–9, p 161 [1379–80]

iii: exile

*The **TRANSLATOR** of the **CHORUS** walks across*
the platform with the UHADI (Calabash Bow) and
sits on the downstage right corner. A woman from the
***CHORUS** seats herself on the upstage left corner behind*
the UMASENGWANA (Milking / Friction Drum). As the
UMNGQOKOLO (Split Tone) singing resolves, the UHADI
*(Calabash Bowing) begins. **ELEKTRA** moves centre stage*
and addresses the audience directly.

ELEKTRA: It is seventeen years since she hacked my
            father like a tree with an axe.
            Wapharhaza intloko kaTata kubini
            ngezembe echitha ubuchopho bakhe
            emhlabeni.
            [HACKED HIS HEAD IN TWO WITH AN AXE – AND
            SPILT HIS BRAINS ONTO THE SOIL.]
            Split his face open with an axe and buried
            his body on the outskirts of the village. I
            saw her and Ayesthus – her lover – dance
            in his blood that night.
            I tried to help him – but I was only a
            child.
            'Tata [FATHER] can you see me? Can you see
            me Tata [FATHER]? Please say yes.'
            I stole my little brother Orestes from his
            bed that night.

KLYTEMNESTRA: (*Looking frantically in the empty blanket*
                 beside the pot.)
                 Orestes?... Orestes?

28

ELEKTRA:	I knew they would kill him too, for his birthright, if I did not send him away.

ELEKTRA pulls the blanket from her shoulders and rolls into a small bundle. This is her infant brother ORESTES – stolen from his bed.

(*Calling urgently into the dark.*)
Mama Nosomething? Mama Nosomething…

One of the women of the CHORUS – Ma NOSOMETHING – stands at the corner of the playing area.

Ma NOSOMETHING:	Ngubani lo undibizayo? [WHO CALLS ME?]
ELEKTRA:	Ndim, ndicela undincede undithathele lo'mtwana toro, umkhulise ngathi ngowakho. [IT IS ME. PLEASE HELP ME! TAKE THIS CHILD FAR FROM HERE AND RAISE HIM LIKE YOUR OWN.]
Ma NOSOMETHING:	Kulungile mntwana wam ndizakumthatha Ndimkhulise de abemmdala. [ALRIGHT MY CHILD. I WILL TAKE HIM FROM HERE AND RAISE HIM UNTIL HE IS GROWN.]

Ma NOSOMETHING steals away into the dark and returns to the other WOMEN of the CHORUS, who gather around the 'child', kissing and touching the bundle.

ELEKTRA:	I gave him to the women of our Tribe to grow him like a tree in the mountains, until he became a man.
	For seventeen years I did not see him.
	I had to live with her.
	I was the wall she beat against every day.

The sound of UMASENGWANA (Milking / Friction Drum), as KLYTEMNESTRA pushes ELEKTRA's face into the pot of water she used to wash her as a child.

iv: interrogation

| KLYTEMNESTRA: | Where is he? |

She pulls her from the water after a long moment.

> Where is my baby?
> What have you done with my boy?

ELEKTRA will not give her mother the information she is seeking. KLYTEMNESTRA pushes her face beneath the water once again. ELEKTRA endures the interrogation with a courage reminiscent of a political resistance fighter. KLYTEMNESTRA turns from ELEKTRA and lights a cigarette.

> [8]And Ham saw the nakedness of his
> father, and told his brethren without. And

---

8   Book of Genesis 9:20–27. The 'curse of Ham' has been used by some to justify racism, systems like Apartheid, and the enslavement of people of Black African ancestry – believed to be descendants of Ham.

> Shem and Japheth went backward; and
> their faces were backward, so that they
> saw not their father's nakedness. And
> when he awoke from his wine, and knew
> what his younger child had done unto
> him. He said…

> (*Reaching out for* **ELEKTRA**'s *hand.*)
> Cursed be your children.

She pushes the burning tip of the cigarette into **ELEKTRA**'s
palm. **ELEKTRA** *screams.*

> The servants of servants shall they be
> unto their brethren. The seed of your
> line shall be the carriers of water and the
> hewers of wood.

Straddling **ELEKTRA**, *she pushes the burning tip into the
side of her daughter's neck.*
Screaming, **ELEKTRA** *tries to crawl away.*

> For the Lord thy God is a jealous God.
> And your dark descendents shall live in
> slavery… All the days of their lives.
> What have you done with my baby?

Exploding with rage at **ELEKTRA**'s *silence.*

> WHERE IS MY SON?

ELEKTRA, *though weeping, will not relent.*
KLYTEMNESTRA *gathers her from the floor and cradles her
daughter.*

(*With grim determination.*)
I'll get it out of you.

v: dreams

KLYTEMNESTRA stands and walks towards her
Testimony Table. She puts out her cigarette as the sound of
UMASENGWANA (Milking / Friction Drum) fades. She
seats herself to testify. She speaks into the mike, directly to
audience.

KLYTEMNESTRA: What is guilt?
What is memory?
What is pain?
Things that wake me in the night...
By day I stand by what I have done
But at night I dream –
And dreams don't lie.

She climbs slowly onto the Testifying Table – which has now
become her bed. She is tormented, twisting in her slumber.
Three WOMEN of the CHORUS rise from their seats. They
move towards her humming an ancient lullaby.

ELEKTRA: (*Addressing the audience directly.*)
I would hear her through the walls each
night...
[9]Dreaming she was giving birth –

---

9   Adapted from *The Libation Bearers* (IJ), l 660 [527]

*The **WOMEN** from the **CHORUS** are the attendant midwives to **KLYTEMNESTRA**. They help her into a squatting position, supporting her from behind.*

MIDWIVES: Pusha! Pusha! [PUSH! PUSH!]

ELEKTRA: But from her womb comes a snake.

*One of the midwives pulls a writhing, blood-covered snake from between **KLYTEMNESTRA**'s legs. They place it on her breast.*

> The midwives wrap it in a blanket and put it on her breast.
> But with her milk it sucks out clots of her blood.

KLYTEMNESTRA screams and starts awake. The house is quiet.

vi: grief

ELEKTRA rolls away from the 'wall' through which she was listening to KLYTEMNESTRA's dream. She stands beside her father's grave.

ELEKTRA: The years pass –
and the grass grows over the grave of a loved one. They told me I was caught in grief.
People said I must just move on.
But how? How could I forget?

How can we move on until the debt is
paid?

ELEKTRA crawls towards her father's grave and lies upon it.

I would hear them at night from my
father's grave.
The voices of the dead whispering
through the years:

The CHORUS softly sings.

'Restore my house.'
'The perpetrator has no right to live
between those walls.'
'Take back what is rightfully ours.'
Somewhere out there was my brother in
exile. But until he returned I could do
nothing…but wait.

*The CHORUS stands and begins a slow dance, circling
ELEKTRA on her father's grave. They seat themselves along
the periphery of the performance space, watching her.*

Kuni nina Zinyanya zakowethu – nina
ningasekhoyo kulomhlaba – Nina
ningasaboniyo ngaliso lanyama…
[TO YOU MY ANCESTORS – YOU WHO ARE NO
LONGER IN THIS WORLD – YOU WHO SEE THINGS
THAT ARE NOT SEEN…]
It is dark. Light my way.
Nini kuphela enaziyo eyona nto
eyenzekayo.

[IT IS YOU ALONE WHO KNOW WHAT TRULY
HAPPENED.]
Send to me – Orestes – my brother – my
blood. Bring him back from exile after
these seventeen years – for
[10]I have no more strength to bear up
alone against the weight of this.

*She nestles into the dark soil of her father's grave, and falls
asleep there.*

vii: grave

*UMASENGWANA (the Milking / Friction Drum) begins
its haunting tempo. KLYTEMNESTRA stands over
Agamemnon's grave – watching ELEKTRA, asleep in
the cemetery soil. KLYTEMNESTRA holds a 'sjambok'
(traditional South African whip made of cured leather). She
cracks the whip. ELEKTRA scrambles from the grave – away
from her mother's quiet, vicious rage.*

KLYTEMNESTRA: (*Softly, with danger.*)
                         Have you been here all night again?
                         Sleeping on that grave?

ELEKTRA: Wenza ntoni?
                         [WHAT ARE YOU DOING HERE?]
                         You have no right to be here!

---

10   *Electra* (Sophocles: RCJ) [119–20]

KLYTEMNESTRA:	[11]You dare speak to me like this – for my husband is not here to keep you from blaming me and straying out of bounds. You come here although you know your father and I have strictly forbidden it.
ELEKTRA:	He is not my father. Ndiyamoyika. Andimhloniphi [I FEAR HIM. I DO NOT RESPECT HIM.] [12]Why do you encourage his violence against me?
KLYTEMNESTRA:	It is his way. You too have a stubborn nature!
ELEKTRA:	Stubborn because I grieve the father I loved?
KLYTEMNESTRA:	Seventeen years you have grieved! The only thing you love is misery.
ELEKTRA:	[13]Only a fool forgets a father's death.
KLYTEMNESTRA:	Your father! Always your father Agamemnon! Nothing else lives in you but the death he got from me. But I had an ally in this- [14]for justice slew him, and not I alone. If you were a mother – you would have done the same. This brutal

11   *Electra* (Sophocles: SU) [622]

12   Adapted from *Electra* (Euripides: EPC) [1116]

13   *Electra* (Sophocles: SU) [144]

14   *Electra* (Sophocles: RCJ) [528]

father of yours, whom you mourn and
mourn, sacrificed your sister –
For some godforsaken Holy War!
He let her die.
[15]He the begetter only with his seed.
For he did not toil for her for nine long
months as I did
– The mother that bore her.

ELEKTRA: It was War! He had no choice.

KLYTEMNESTRA: We all have choice. And I made mine.
I took what was owed me:
Breath for breath, and life for life.
[16]And so would say your dead sister, if
she could speak.
[17]Let Agamemnon make no great boasts
in the halls of Hell. For he has paid for
what he first began.

ELEKTRA: Ngamthetho wuphi? [BY WHAT LAW?]

KLYTEMNESTRA: By the justice of a mother.

ELEKTRA: Were Orestes and I not also born of your
womb?
My brother would have died too by your
lover's hand that night, if I had not sent
him away.

---

15   Adapted from *Electra* (Sophocles: DG), ll 534–5, p 146 [533]

16   *Electra* (Sophocles: SU) [548]

17   Clytemnestra in *Agamemnon* (SU) [1528–9]

And now all these years I am forced to
serve in the Halls of my Father's House.
Is my dead sister the only one to know
your Justice as a mother?

KLYTEMNESTRA: [18]She begged him: 'Do not kill me before
my time. Don't force me to gaze at
darkness in the world below.'

ELEKTRA: It was the price of war.

KLYTEMNESTRA: Until you have borne a child – don't you
dare talk to me about the price of war.

ELEKTRA: Yes! My womb remains empty and I am
without child.
The man who sleeps in my father's bed
has forbidden any man to come near me
– for fear that I will breed a son who will
some day avenge my father's death.
But Agamemnon's line will not die.
My brother lives.
Seventeen years ago – he was a child. But
time passes.
And the boy is now a man.

KLYTEMNESTRA: A man? And where is this man who
promises to come…
But never resolves.

ELEKTRA: He will come!
Uyazi ukuba uza kuza [YOU KNOW HE WILL!]

---

18   Iphigenia to Agamemnon. Euripides, *Iphigenia in Aulis* (SU) [1219]

And you fear it.
Every night you wait for his shadow to
fall over your bed. You are dreaming of
him again....

KLYTEMNESTRA: (*Startled.*) Who told you that?

ELEKTRA: I hear your fear at night through the
walls.
I see you coming to pay penance each
year at your victim's grave? You think no
one knows you.
But I see your heart.
I know it hurts.

KLYTEMNESTRA: I am done here. (*Turning to go.*)

ELEKTRA: You loved me once, I think.
You loved my brother – and you loved
me...

*ELEKTRA starts to weep. KLYTEMNESTRA falters for
a moment.*

Mama, if I speak gently – can I say my
truth?

KLYTEMNESTRA: (*Casting aside her 'sjambok' and coming to
her.*)
[19]Indeed, you have my leave.

---

19   *Electra* (Sophocles: RCJ) [556–7]

> And if you always addressed me in such a
> gentle tone, you would be heard without
> pain.

ELEKTRA grasps her legs, kneeling before her.

ELEKTRA: I want only to know you.
Who you were before the hurting…
who we could have been.

KLYTEMNESTRA: [20]I am not so exceeding glad at the deeds
that I have done…

ELEKTRA: I know. And I know you wish it could
have been different, but you breed with
him, and honor his line, while you cast us
out - your true children.
Yonke lento uyenzela isiqu sakho – Hayi
intombi yakho ebuleweyo!
[ALL OF THIS YOU ARE DOING FOR YOURSELF – NOT
FOR YOUR MURDERED DAUGHTER!]
Taking night after night…the man who
has my father's blood on his hands –
Kule nyo yakho! [INTO YOUR CUNT!]
You are nothing but that man's Bitch.

*KLYTEMNESTRA, enraged, charges at ELEKTRA with
the whip. ELEKTRA runs in terror and hides behind the
CHORUS of WOMEN. They raise their arms to protect her,
and she huddles behind them. KLYTEMNESTRA speaks to
all.*

---

20   *Electra* (Euripides: EPC) [1106]

KLYTEMNESTRA: Let me tell you about this Bitch – and how she met the man you call father.

There are things you do not know about me child: A history that was written long before you were born.

I too was happy once.

I was not always Klytemnestra who carried this curse.

Before your father – I was married to a man I loved – with a child – my first born.

The power in that bond you will never know.

A woman giving birth is an animal in pain.

Hurt her child – and the wound is hers... Cuts her where she cannot heal.

I met your father the day he opened up my first husband and ripped out his guts. [21]He tore this – my firstborn from my breast. Then holding the child by its new ankles – he smashed its tiny head against a rock. Then took me for his wife.

Ah! My daughter, he that begat you murdered more than one of my children. For well you know – years later he would slit your own sister's throat as a sacrifice for peace.

PEACE? WHOSE PEACE?

It is an old and terrible world, and I feel its pain.

---

21   Source unknown

	But if you ever dare speak to me like that again,
	I will answer you from my black heart.
	For it is not I who first taught you to be so base.

ELEKTRA: [22]Base deeds are taught by base.
If you find me accomplished in such things...
It is because I am my mother's daughter.

KLYTEMNESTRA: [23]I and my deeds give you too much matter for words.

ELEKTRA: [24]The words are thine – not mine.
For yours is the act – and the act finds its utterance.

KLYTEMNESTRA: I have lived a long time my daughter.
Eye for an eye, blood for blood, and a tooth for a tooth.
It is and will always be men's only truth.

Suddenly, ELEKTRA grabs the 'sjambok' from KLYTEMNESTRA's hand.

ELEKTRA: (*With danger.*)
[25]Take care in making such a law for men,
that you not make trouble for yourself.

22   *Electra* (Sophocles: RCJ) [621]

23   *Electra* (Sophocles: RCJ) [622–3]

24   *Electra* (Sophocles: RCJ) [624–5]

25   Adapted from *Electra* (Sophocles: RCJ) [581–2]

For, if we are to take blood for blood,
then by that law... Wena! [YOU]

In an open threat, she points at her with the 'sjambok'.

You would be the first to die.

*Mother and daughter stare at each other. The danger is
now out in the open. KLYTEMNESTRA turns her back on
ELEKTRA, as the WOMEN break into UMNGQOKOLO
(Split-Tone Singing). KLYTEMNESTRA walks away and
ELEKTRA watches her, standing her ground.*

viii: wet bag method

*KLYTEMNESTRA moves centre stage with her chair raised,
upside down, above her head. The effect is of an animal
with horns, under threat. She turns the chair, places it and
sits. ELEKTRA walks to the table, sits and speaks into the
microphone, directly to her perpetrator.*

ELEKTRA: (*Testimony.*) Years passed between us.
Mother and daughter.
But I was not permitted to sit at the table.
You fed me like a dog.
I was a servant in the halls of my father's
house.
No-one ever talks about the night you
spilled my father's blood.
It is as though the past never happened.
But a daughter remembers.

Sisiyatha sodwa esingalibala ukubulawa
kuka tata waso.
[ONLY A FOOL WOULD FORGET HER FATHER'S
MURDER.]
Every day you tried to break my strength.
Everyday you tried to destroy my spirit.

She comes out from behind her table and stands before a
seated KLYTEMNESTRA.

Please, demonstrate for this commission
how you tried to get information out of
me as to my brother's whereabouts.

ELEKTRA turns her back to KLYTEMNESTRA and lies,
belly down, in front of her. KLYTEMNESTRA moves to
ELEKTRA and straddles her. She takes a plastic bag from her
pocket, places it over ELEKTRA's head, and pulls it tightly.
ELEKTRA begins to suffocate.
This form of torture should be a direct visual reference to the
'Wet Bag Method' – graphically demonstrated at the Truth
Commission, and used by South African Security Police to
torture political activists during the Apartheid regime's rule.
This suffocation should be performed for longer than the
audience would be comfortable with. As ELEKTRA starts
to lose consciousness, and her desperate kicking fades –
KLYTEMNESTRA suddenly pulls the bag from her head.
ELEKTRA gasps for breath.

(*Sobbing with rage.*)
One day you will face your God. And
ask forgiveness for the things you did in
those years…

KLYTEMNESTRA: There was so much fear in those years.
Every night the shadow of my son would fall over my bed.
The inevitable vengeance he would one day bring.
For those we harm as children –
Grow up to be men.

ix: initiation

*The **CHORUS**, in full voice, sings the traditional song for young Xhosa men returning from their initiation in the mountains. **ORESTES** is wrapped, and with his face shrouded, in the striking white and red initiate's blanket, holding a stick over his shoulder. He moves with slow grace towards the centre of the performance area. The **CHORUS** seat themselves in a circle around **ORESTES**. The **WOMAN** who took him, as an infant from **ELEKTRA**, steps forward to praise him and offer the traditional WORDS OF WISDOM.*

WOMAN: [26]Uyindoda ngoku, hamba uyokukhathalela udade wenu.

[NOW THAT YOU ARE A MAN – GO AND TAKE CARE OF YOUR SISTER.]

Hamba uyokwenza izinto zobudoda.

[GO AND DO MANLY THINGS.]

Hamba uyokukhathalela usapho lwakho.

[GO AND TAKE CARE OF YOUR FAMILY.]

---

26 Traditional words of wisdom during a Xhosa initiation adapted by NoSomething Ntese for our story's purposes.

Hamba uyokukhulisa usapho, wakhe nendlu yakho.

[GO RAISE A FAMILY AND BUILD YOUR HOUSE.]

Hamba uyokuthatha ilifa, kunye nendawo yakho.

[GO TAKE YOUR INHERITANCE AND YOUR RIGHTFUL POSITION.]

Izinyanya zakho zifuna ubuyele endlwini kayihlo, uthathe indawo yakho.

[YOUR ANCESTORS WANT YOU TO RETURN TO YOUR FATHER'S HOUSE AND TAKE YOUR POSITION THERE.]

Buya ezintabeni, ujongis'umbomb'ekhaya.

[YOU MUST RETURN FROM THE MOUNTAINS TO GO HOME.]

Zanga iZinyanya zingahamba nawe.

[THE ANCESTORS GO WITH YOU.]

ORESTES stands and drops his blanket to reveal his powerful, muscular physique. We see the boy is now a man. He takes up his new blanket and begins the slow, graceful 'Dance of the Bull'. The **WOMEN** *of the* **CHORUS** *ululate. They sing rapturously, and encircle him – bumping him (as tradition dictates) to test his strength. The* **WOMEN** *of the* **CHORUS** *break into stick fighting and ululate as* **ORESTES** *slowly makes his way forward and away from the mountain he has grown up on. They wave to him and resume their places on their chairs, as Witnesses to the testimonies.* **ORESTES** *walks the perimeter of the performance platform. He has begun the journey of return to his ancestral home.*

ELEKTRA: (*As testimony into the microphone.*)
                              It falls softly: the spirit of revenge.

[27]The brooding Fury finally comes –
leading a child inside the house
to cleanse the stain of blood from long
ago.

KLYTEMNESTRA: (*Testimony.*) I am not so exceeding glad
at the deeds I have done. But we were a
country at war.
It mattered only that we survived.
I had lived so long with the dark figure of
vengeance beneath the bed…
That I suspected nothing the night he
arrived at my door, carrying a tin of ash
and pretending his own death.
We who have done harm to the fathers of
this generation –
We know –
Consequence will arrive –
One dark night –
Unannounced –
At the door.

x: ash

A series of drum beats signal a knocking at the door of
KLYTEMNESTRA's home.
ELEKTRA appears in a shaft of light, with a kerosene lantern
in her hand. Her mother stands behind her.

---

27   *The Libation Bearers* (IJ), ll 808, 810–12 [649–51]

ORESTES: (*Shrouded in his blanket.*)
                     Ingaba ngumzi ka Agamemnon lo?
                     [IS THIS THE HOUSE OF AGAMEMNON?]

KLYTEMNESTRA: No Stranger.
                     You are not from these parts or you
                     would know:
                     For many years now – this is the house of
                     Ayesthus and Klytemnestra.

ORESTES: Does Ayesthus, the man of the house,
                     welcome strangers?

KLYTEMNESTRA: (*Suspiciously.*)
                     [28]What country are you from? Who are
                     you?

ORESTES: Announce me to the masters of the
                     house.
                     I've come to bring them news of Orestes.
                     Khawuleza mama! [HURRY UP MAMA.]
                     Night's black chariot is speeding
                     overhead.
                     And it is a long walk home.

KLYTEMNESTRA: We live under the eyes of Justice here.
                     But if your work is serious, men's work,
                     then we must wait for Ayesthus.
                     He is away – but returns late tonight.

Both women turn back to the house.

---

28   Servant in *The Libation Bearers* (IJ), l 819 [657]

ORESTES: I have a message for the mother of
                      Orestes.

They both stop in their tracks and turn back to face the
stranger.

                      Her son is dead.

*A strike of the drum. **KLYTEMNESTRA** gasps in shock.*

ELEKTRA: (*Screams.*) NO!

ORESTES: Here are his ashes –
                      With whom should I leave them?

ELEKTRA, hearing of the ashes, starts from her grief.

KLYTEMNESTRA: (*Recovering from her shock to prevent*
                      ***ELEKTRA** from claiming the ashes.*)
                      I am the mother of Orestes.
                      You may leave them with me.

*The **CHORUS** begins the ephemeral sound of the UMRUHE*
*(Mouth Bows) as **KLYTEMNESTRA** reaches for the ashes.*
She opens the tin and lets her son's supposed remains pour
through her fingers.

                      [29]Now I know – the stock of our ancient
                      masters is perished, root and branch. And
                      the ancient bloodline is blotted out.

ELEKTRA suddenly lunges for the tin and the two women
struggle fiercely.

---

29   Adapted from Chorus' words in *Electra* (Sophocles: RCJ) [764–5]

ELEKTRA overpowers her mother, pulling the tin from her.
She falls into ORESTES' arms.
He holds her for a moment. She pushes him and runs.

Excuse my daughter.
She is in love with misery.

ORESTES turns to look at her.

What?
It must seem strange for me not to grieve
the death of my only son. [30]But he, who
sprang from my own life, has been the
terror of my dreams. Neither by night
nor day has sweet sleep covered my eyes.
From moment to moment I have lived
in the shadow of death. Time's prisoner
condemned, to wait for my own murder.
Now this day I am finally rid of the threat
of him. And her!
That serpent sucking out my heart's red
wine.
Now at last my children are silenced…
and peace is mine!

ORESTES: I must give this news directly to the man
                   of the house.

KLYTEMNESTRA: My husband returns after midnight.
                   But you are welcome to wait here,
                   Stranger, and eat with us tonight.

_____

30   *Electra* (Sophocles: RCJ) [775]

ORESTES:	Ndiyabulela ngempatho yakho entle.
	[THANK YOU FOR YOUR GENEROSITY.]
	I have some business in town – but will be back after dark.

KLYTEMNESTRA:	Come when you are ready.
	Tonight – my home is yours.

ORESTES smiles fleetingly and then turns and goes.
KLYTEMNESTRA turns back to the house, but for a moment feels a presence out in the dark.
She raises her lantern.

Who's there?

The CHORUS of WOMEN walk towards the edges of the stage, looking at KLYTEMNESTRA.
The sound of ISITOLO-TOLO (Jew's Harp) accompanies them.
She turns and retreats into the house.

xi: found

ELEKTRA is lying on her father's grave. She is inconsolable with grief.

ELEKTRA:	Tata, uOrestes usishiyile!
	[PAPA, ORESTES HAS LEFT US!]
	Ngoluthuthu ndikhalela ilizwe lam.
	[WITH THESE ASHES I CRY FOR MY NATION.]
	Ndikuthanda ngentliziyo yam yonke.
	[I LOVED YOU WITH ALL MY HEART.]

Orestes – you died alone in exile – kude nekhaya [FAR FROM HOME].

These loving hands could not wash your corpse, could not help to lift you into the fire.

Isidumbu sakho sahlanjwa zizandla ongazaziyo.

[YOUR CORPSE WAS CLEANED AND PREPARED BY THE HANDS OF STRANGERS.]

Phupho lam, themba lam,

[MY DREAM, MY HOPE,]

Our future is now ash.

Ikamva lethu luthuthu!

[OUR FUTURE IS ASH!]

Ndithathe khon'ukuze ndibe nawe.

[TAKE ME SO THAT I WILL BE WITH YOU.]

Take me as nothing, into your nothingness, that I may live with you – Emgodini [IN THE GROUND].

Kuba emhlabeni besimntu mnye, nasekufeni makube njalo.

[BECAUSE ON EARTH WE WERE ONE, EVEN IN DEATH LET IT BE SO.]

She hears someone coming and – fearing it is her mother
– hides behind the **CHORUS** *of* **WOMEN,** *seated*
along the periphery of the earthen floor. The sound of
UMASENGWANA (Milking / Friction Drum) begins.
Entering the cemetery is the stranger who brought **ELEKTRA**
the ashes of her brother. Throwing off his blanket, he kneels at
her father's grave. He spits traditional beer in honour of the

Ancestors, and lights Mphepo (the herb that is burnt when communing with the Ancestors).

ORESTES: Kuwe lizwe lam, nakuni Zinyanya.
[TO YOU MY COUNTRY AND TO YOU MY ANCESTORS.]
[31]Receive me with good fortune in this journey.
Halls of my fathers,
Kuba ndize apha ukuza kufezekisa isenzo esibalulekileyo.
[I HAVE COME HERE TO FULFIL AN IMPORTANT TASK.]
Send me not dishonoured from the land, but grant that I take back what is mine, and restore my house!
Ndiyanibongoza, sebenzisanani nam.
[PLEASE, WORK WITH ME.]
Now I've come back to this land from seventeen years of exile – a man. And I swear on this grave:
Ngeke ndibuyele emva ndingakhange ndiziphindisele.
[I WILL NOT RETURN WITHOUT MY REVENGE.]

He turns to go. ELEKTRA steps out from the shadows.

ELEKTRA: (*Breathless.*) Orestes?

He turns to her and they look at each other for a long moment.

---

31   *Electra* (Sophocles: RCJ) [68]

uOrestes?

He nods gently. She steps away from him, afraid. He moves towards her.

Ngeke! [NEVER!] My brother is dead!
You are the one who brought us his ashes!

ORESTES: My sister…dade wethu [MY SISTER] – it is me.
I still have the stone you gave me as a child.

ORESTES takes the stone from his pocket. Tentatively she steps towards him and snatches it. She looks at it and falls to her knees.
They embrace for a long moment as she weeps, first in rage and then in joy.

ELEKTRA: Orestes… Orestes…
Let me look at you. Let me look at your face.
Ungumfanekiso ka yihlo uAgamemnon.
[YOU ARE THE IMAGE OF AGAMEMNON.]
You are your father's son.
[32]Here is Orestes that was dead in craft.
And now by craft restored to life again.
Child of the body that I loved best, at last you have found me.
You have found those you yearned for.

---

32   *Electra* (Sophocles: SU) [1228–9]

The CHORUS begins the pulse of IGUBU (the Traditional
Drum). ELEKTRA and ORESTES circle the grave.

> (*Proudly to her brother.*)
> Ntsika yesizwe sethu.
> [TO YOU THE PILLAR OF THE NATION.]
> [33]The seed of hope through all our
> weeping. Trust your own strength and
> win back again your father's house.

ORESTES: Zinyanya zakowethu khanyisani indlela.
Ityala eli kweli ngcwaba likhalela
impindezelo…
[MY ANCESTORS LIGHT THE WAY. THE CRIME IN
THIS GRAVE CRIES OUT FOR JUSTICE]
Let it be done. [34]One murderous stroke
is paid off by another lethal blow. So runs
the ancient curse, now three generations
old.

Two of the WOMEN of the CHORUS play UMRUBHE
(Mouth Bow). The others beat a pulse with their hands on
the floor and hum. ELEKTRA circles the grave, as ORESTES
spits beer over the sacred soil. The following is chanted
– building in intensity.

ELEKTRA: Father that begot us…
[35]Among the dead the savage jaws of fire
cannot destroy the spirit.
Father that begot us…

33   *The Libation Bearers* (IJ), ll 296–8 [236]

34   Chorus in *The Libation Bearers* (IJ), ll 379–80, 382–3 [312–13, 314]

35   Chorus in *The Libation Bearers* (IJ), ll 393–4 [323–4]

Bawo wethu....sive

[OUR FATHER...HEAR US NOW]

[36]As, in turn, we mourn and weep.

Your two children at your tomb now sing your death song.

[37]Orphans...see us like this both outcasts.

Banished from our home.

Yiba nathi, usincede siphakamise igama lakho.

[BE WITH US AND HELP US TO HONOUR YOUR NAME.]

ORESTES: Father that begot us...

Lord of the world below, see the survivors of our father's line.

Silapha njengeenkedama, singenancedo nakhaya.

[WE ARE HERE AS ORPHANS WITHOUT HELP OR HOME.]

ELEKTRA: Mother that betrayed us...

Isikhohlakali somama

[MOST TERRIBLE MOTHER]

[38]You dared place him in a tomb without the rites of mourning.

ELEKTRA and ORESTES keep moving fluidly around the grave and each other, as the intensity builds.

---

36   *The Libation Bearers* (IJ), ll 404–6 [332–5]

37   *The Libation Bearers* (IJ), ll 311, 315–16 [247, 253–4]

38   *The Libation Bearers* (IJ), ll 533–4 [432–4]

39You first hacked off his limbs, wazigaxa emqaleni wakhe,

[AND YOU HUNG THEM ON HIS NECK,]

then hung them round his neck. That's how you buried him.

Mother that betrayed us…you made my father's death an abomination.

Wandihlaza [YOU SHAMED ME] and set me apart inside a cell, as if I were some rabid dog.

Ndarhayiza! [I WAILED!] I wept. I died.

She falls into **ORESTES**' *arms and then moves out addressing both the audience and* **CHORUS**.

All who pay attention to this house of trouble hear these words.

Carve them on your heart that we may never forget.

ORESTES: Ungalibali Tata, ungalibali Thongo lam

[DO NOT FORGET FATHER, DO NOT FORGET MY ANCESTOR]

40that night that you were slaughtered.

The **CHORUS** *responds with a chanting refrain.*

CHORUS: Makubenjalo! [LET IT BE SO!]

ELEKTRA: Ungalibali Tata, ungalibali Thongo lam.

---

39   *The Libation Bearers* [paraphrase] (IJ), ll 540–55 [439–40]

40   *The Libation Bearers* (IJ), l 618 [491]

[DO NOT FORGET FATHER, DO NOT FORGET MY ANCESTORS.]

[41]The net in which they killed you.

CHORUS:	Makubenjalo! [LET IT BE SO!]

ELEKTRA:	Ungalibali Tata, ungalibali Thongo lam. [42]When they covered you with deceit and shame.

CHORUS:	Makubenjalo! [LET IT BE SO!]

ORESTES:	Tata sibiza wena. [FATHER WE ARE CALLING YOU.] Stand by your children.

ELEKTRA:	[43]Through these tears I join his call. In unison, our voices blend as one – hear us. Yiba nathi xa silwayo neentshaba zethu. [BE WITH US IN FIGHTING OUR ENEMIES.] Umthetho mawuvelise inyaniso. [LET JUSTICE REVEAL THE TRUTH.]

CHORUS:	Makubenjalo! [LET IT BE SO!]

ORESTES:	Father, make me the master of your house.

---

41   *The Libation Bearers* (IJ), l 619 [492]

42   *The Libation Bearers* (IJ), l 622–3 [494]

43   *The Libation Bearers* (IJ), l 573 [457]

[44]Once drops of blood are shed upon the
ground they cry out for more.

CHORUS: Makubenjalo, kubechosi kube hele!!
[LET IT BE SO!]

All instrumentation, humming and rhythms cease.

ELEKTRA: [45]So let the one who bore us grovel.
We're bred from her, like wolves, whose
savage hearts do not relent.

*A **WOMAN** of the **CHORUS** plays the INKINGE (Bow With
Five Litre Tin Can Resonator) and the **WOMEN** surround
ORESTES and **ELEKTRA**, as they play at being wolves
together – rolling sensuously in the sand and on one another.*

xii: plan

*KLYTEMNESTRA walks through the **WOMEN** and crosses
the stage. She mutters to herself, smoking with one hand – a
bottle of whiskey in the other.*

KLYTEMNESTRA: (*To herself.*) [46]I was your chaste and
faithful wife; yet I must lose my daughter,
while the whore Helen could keep her
daughter and live safe and flourishing at
home…

---

44   *The Libation Bearers* (IJ), ll 493–4 [400–2]

45   Adapted from *The Libation Bearers* (SU), ll 516–17 [420–2]

46   Clytemnestra to Agamemnon, Euripides, *Iphigenia in Aulis* (SU) [1204]

She stops suddenly – thinking she has heard something. The
***CHORUS** ceases their music and foot stamping for a beat.*
She looks around in fear. She moves away. The rhythms
resume.

ORESTES: [47]My plan is simple.
                   I'm expected at our mother's table
                   after dark. Though she knows me as a
                   stranger – we will eat as a family tonight.

ELEKTRA: She will be drunk before the night is out.

ORESTES: I will lay her to bed like a child in the
                   womb…
                   And wait for our stepfather's return.
                   She will see me rip his heart from its cage.
                   And then I will open her in our father's
                   bed.

ELEKTRA: She dreams every night she gives birth to
                   a snake.

ORESTES: [48]I come from the same womb as that
                   snake.
                   This dream fulfils itself in me.
                   She will die by violence for she has
                   nursed a violent thing.

*The **CHORUS** of **WOMEN** break into the song ITHONGO*
LAM [MY ANCESTORS LEAD ME].

---

47   *The Libation Bearers* (IJ), l 691 [554]

48   Adapted from *The Libation Bearers* (IJ), l 679 [543]

ORESTES dances, as ELEKTRA runs home to prepare for the coming night.
The CHORUS move to the table stage right, upon which KLYTEMNESTRA sits. They lift the table and move it stage centre with KLYTEMNESTRA borne aloft. A sacrificial lamb? A drunken Queen in her chariot? The CHORUS surrounds the table in a half circle, as KLYTEMNESTRA, behind this human curtain, climbs from the table.
The CHORUS move back to their seats dancing and singing – as ORESTES and KLYTEMNESTRA are seated and KLYTEMNESTRA lights the candles.

xiii: home

All singing stops and in the silence, and we hear the sound of tearing flesh, as KLYTEMNESTRA divides a roast chicken and serves herself and ORESTES generous portions.
She has been drinking and is clearly inebriated, though still perfectly in control.

KLYTEMNESTRA: (*She places a minute potion of food on a plate for ELEKTRA.*) Tata! [TAKE!]

ELEKTRA is cleaning sodden clothes in a basin nearby. She takes the food and returns to her seated position on the floor, to eat. KLYTEMNESTRA notices ORESTES watching this with emotion.

> Let her not move you!
> She weeps not for the news of her
> brother!

She grieves the loss of her revenge!

KLYTEMNESTRA tears the chicken's leg.

Something else to eat?

ORESTES: Ndiyabulela mama! [THANK YOU MA!]

KLYTEMNESTRA: (*Hissing at ELEKTRA.*)
Hang it up to dry!

*ELEKTRA pulls from the bowl of washing, an enormous
male labourer's uniform. She hangs it on a hook. It conjures
the shape of its owner: Ayesthus. The sheer size of it indicates
the intimidating and enormous physical presence he holds
in the house. His boots – equally gargantuan – wait beside
ELEKTRA, to be polished.*

My husband went to see his mother for
month end.
But stay as late as you need. Ayesthus will
be pleased to meet the man who brought
home the ashes of my son.

BOOTS!

*ELEKTRA removes her boots for her. KLYTEMNESTRA
suddenly grabs ELEKTRA by the arm.*

Speak all that is in your heart, and tell me
that your father's death was not deserved.

*She releases ELEKTRA from her grip and lights a cigarette,
lost in her drunken thoughts.*

ELEKTRA and ORESTES exchange glances. ELEKTRA places her mother's boots beside the boots of Ayesthus, and begins to polish.

How many children can a mother lose?
First it was my baby he smashed against a rock.
Then Ephigenia – sacrificed like a goat.
And now Orestes – gone!

ORESTES: I have heard this story in the village.
Wenza ntoni wena ke mama? [WHAT DID YOU DO MA? ('MA' AS A MEANS OF ADDRESSING AN OLDER WOMAN WITH RESPECT, RATHER THAN LITERALLY 'MOTHER'.)]
How did you take your revenge?

KLYTEMNESTRA: I took a lover…

Pointing to the suspended uniform.

Ayesthus! [49]And planned to welcome my husband home – not with crown or garland…
but with a sharpened axe.

KLYTEMNESTRA stands, to re-enact the scene.

[50]When my conquering husband returned…

49   Electra in *Electra* (Sophocles: SU) [163–4]

50   Source unknown

We lit fires throughout the city, feigning
celebrations. Crimson tapestries were laid
between Agamemnon and the entrance of
our home.
And reaching towards him I whispered
for the whole city to hear:
'Come to me now my love, down from
the car of war, but step upon these
tapestries we have lain to honour your
coming home. Those feet that have
stamped out our enemies need never
touch earth again, my great one.'

*She picks up the enormous boots and walks them along the
edge of the table, conjuring Agamemnon's last steps.*

And they never did.
(*Simply.*) We killed him dead.

*She throws the boots to the ground to the thump of IGUBU
(the Drum).*

That was the last night I saw my boy –
Orestes.
Seventeen years I had not seen him.
And now…never more.

*KLYTEMNESTRA takes a small pair of shoes from her
pocket that once belonged to ORESTES. A WOMAN of the
CHORUS sings softly. KLYTEMNESTRA begins to cry.
ORESTES is visibly moved.*

[51]Girl – It was ever your nature to love your father...
But sons have a deeper affection for their mothers...
And mothers for their sons.
As a babe – I could not wean him from the breast.
He was just a little boy when she took him away.
(*Addressing the shoes.*) Orestes...
I never saw you a man.

ELEKTRA: (*Sensing **ORESTES'** sudden emotion, steps between them.*)
She has no right to use my brother's name.

KLYTEMNESTRA: (*In **ELEKTRA**'s ear, with renewed cruelty.*)
Ayesthus and I danced in your father's blood...

*KLYTEMNESTRA takes the arms of the hanging uniform and dances, as a **WOMAN** from the **CHORUS** plays a jaunty tune on IFLEYITI (Harmonica).*
*Returning to **ELEKTRA**, she stands inches from her.*

We revealed your father's broken body for all to see.
'Here lies Agamemnon, my husband, made a corpse by this right hand – a masterpiece of Justice. Done is done.'

---

51   Adapted from *Electra* (Euripides: EPC) [1102–3]

She sits heavily, unable to support herself. She is now terribly drunk.

(*Slurring.*) Done is done! Done is done...

*The playing of IFLEYITI (Harmonica) resumes, as KLYTEMNESTRA sways to the music and then passes out cold. Three WOMEN from the CHORUS step forward. One stands behind KLYTEMNESTRA and begins to play ISITOLO-TOLO (Jew's Harp). The two other WOMEN of the CHORUS come around the table to look at KLYTEMNESTRA. They chuckle between themselves. ELEKTRA removes the cigarette from her mother's hand. KLYTEMNESTRA starts awake to find ORESTES standing over her. He holds out his arms and she obliges like a child. He lifts her in his arms and makes to carry her to her bed – but not before she leans back to snatch her whiskey bottle from the table. He lays her on her Testimony Table, where the WOMEN of the CHORUS wait.
ELEKTRA climbs onto the table with the axe in her hand for the first time.*

ELEKTRA: [52]If you prick us – do we not bleed?
                     If you tickle us – do we not laugh?
                     If you poison us – do we not die?
                     And if you wrong us...
                     Shall we not revenge?

ORESTES returns to the table. ELEKTRA pulls him towards her.

---

52   *The Merchant of Venice* by William Shakespeare, III.i, ll 49–61

If you go now – you will find Ayesthus
crossing the field towards the house.
Slaughter him like a beast and bring me
his heart.

ORESTES: Father that begot us…
Lord of the world below, see the survivors
of our father's line.
Silapha njengeenkedama singenancedo
nakhaya.
[WE ARE HERE AS ORPHANS WITHOUT HELP OR
HOME.]

ELEKTRA: [53] As there is justice in Heaven.

*IGUBU (A drum beat) from the **CHORUS**.*
***ELEKTRA** and **ORESTES** climb onto the table and stand
with arms spread to the Heavens.*

And fire in the hands of the gods.
Our reckoning must be made.
Umhlaba mawuxelele abaphantsi ukuba
siyeza.
[THE EARTH SHOULD TELL OUR ANCESTORS THAT
WE ARE COMING.]
Here we come.
The tide is turning at last.

***ORESTES** jumps from the table and, with weapon in
hand, sets out for the field to find Ayesthus. The actor walks
the full periphery of the stage, in a stylized, protracted*

---

53   Source unknown

*manner. The **WOMEN** of the **CHORUS**, smoking their pipes,*
watch him go.

xiv: curse

ELEKTRA moves to the uniform of Ayesthus. She removes
it from its hook, throws it to the ground and spits on it.
KLYTEMNESTRA starts awake. ELEKTRA disappears
beneath the table.

KLYTEMNESTRA: (*Suddenly up with a stick in her hand.*)
                  Who's there?

She is off the bed and moving towards the 'kitchen' again.
*A **WOMAN** of the **CHORUS** is softly Beat Dancing*
– creating a rhythm with her feet. She stands beside
*KLYTEMNESTRA, who cannot see her. **KLYTEMNESTRA***
notices the uniform on the ground.

                  Ayesthus – are you home?

With her back turned, ELEKTRA hangs a large dead snake
behind KLYTEMNESTRA and slips back beneath the table.
KLYTEMNESTRA turns to see the snake and screams. The
CHORUS WOMAN intensifies the rhythmic movement
of her feet. IGUBU (the Traditional Drum) assumes the
quickening of the rhythm, like a heartbeat that is racing.
KLYTEMNESTRA lights Mphepho (herb that is burnt when
communing with the Ancestors).
She smothers the dead animal in the smoke – in an attempt
to neutralise the curse that has been put on her House.

Hamba Moyomube! Hamba Satan!

[AWAY EVIL SPIRITS! AWAY SATAN!]

She stands with stick in hand and calls out.

I am from the house of Atreus!
I fear none!

*The **WOMEN** of the **CHORUS** move into the space, singing.*
They clear all set elements.

xv: vengeance

*Out in the field, **ORESTES** breaks into a run. As the*
***CHORUS** sings, **ORESTES'** feet lift from the ground.*
Suspended (by stage device) he continues his long strides
towards his destiny. He lifts the pickaxe and swings it above
his head. His body is carried by the weight of the weapon, in
fluid circular motions – until he strikes violently at Ayesthus'
boots centre stage. The boots, filled with blood, spill their
*contents across the stage. **ORESTES** tears a large heart*
from one of the boots and stumbles backwards. One of the
***WOMEN** of the **CHORUS**, who raised him, appears to him.*
He is unsure if she is real or a vision. He drops to his knees
stunned.

Ma NOSOMETHING: Mntwan'am! Kutheni ubulala nje?

[MY CHILD! WHY DO YOU KILL?]

Umntu akabulawa.

[A HUMAN BEING SHOULD NEVER BE MURDERED.]

Uyalazi ukuba igazi lomntu liya
kukumangalela?

[DO YOU KNOW THAT HUMAN BLOOD WILL HAUNT
YOU ALWAYS?]

Imbi lento uyenzayo.

[WHAT YOU HAVE DONE IS TERRIBLE]

Ungaze uphinde ubulale. [NEVER KILL AGAIN.]

ORESTES reaches for her but she is gone.

xvi: lost

ELEKTRA: Orestes…? Orestes…?

*ELEKTRA is crawling through the field, looking for her
brother.*

ORESTES: Ndikuphathele yonke into owake
                    wayifuna…
                    [I HAVE BROUGHT YOU ALL THAT YOU EVER
                    WANTED…]

*He lifts the heart towards her. She takes it from him and
starts to laugh and then weep. She puts Ayesthus' boots on
and dances wildly.*

ELEKTRA: At last – Ayesthus, you are what you
                    always were…
                    an animal without a heart.
                    And now s'thandwa sami [DARLING] – for
                    the greater deed.
                    She is asleep in our father's bed.
                    Open her tonight and finally set us free.

ORESTES:	Elektra – we are lost!
ELEKTRA:	(*Stunned for a moment, but recovering instantly.*) Famous spirit of Revenge – you have done your ancestors proud! Ungalibali Tata, ungalibali Thongo lam! [DO NOT FORGET MY FATHER, DO NOT FORGET MY ANCESTOR!]
ORESTES:	That night that he was slaughtered.
ELEKTRA:	Ungalibali Tata, ungalibali Thongo lam. [DO NOT FORGET MY FATHER, DO NOT FORGET MY ANCESTOR!] How they covered you with deceit and shame.
ORESTES:	Tata sibiza wena. [FATHER WE ARE CALLING YOU] Stand by your children. [54]By the gods – by my own hand, Let me kill my mother – then let me die.

xvii: truth

*There is a strike of the drum. **ELEKTRA** and **ORESTES** turn to find **KLYTEMNESTRA** standing behind them. She is staring wildly at **ORESTES**.*

---

54   Source unknown

KLYTEMNESTRA: Of course – the dark face of Agamemnon.
My son, my child, Orestes – raised from
the dead.
At last in the flesh.
Not the stranger with the ashes – or the
shadow over my bed…but a man before
me, carrying the face of my darkest
nights.

ELEKTRA: The man you spread your legs for in my
father's bed…
Nantsi intliziyo yakhe –
[HERE IS HIS HEART]
You have his heart…

She places the heart at her mother's feet.

Thatha! [HERE!]
Do with it as you will!

KLYTEMNESTRA: (*Screams in agony, falling to her knees.*)
NO!
[55]My love, my power…
Dead.

ELEKTRA: [56]By whose side you soon will lie as a
corpse and you shall be his bride in Hell's
halls as wife you were to him on earth.

KLYTEMNESTRA: You stupid girl, you witless child –
You know not what you do.

---

55   Adapted from *The Libation Bearers* (IJ), l 1110 [893]

56   Adapted from *Electra* (Euripides: EPC) [1144–5]

Already the darkness is in your eyes.
You become me. You choose the curse.

ELEKTRA circles KLYTEMNESTRA dangerously.

ELEKTRA: Ndikhetha isiqalekiso?
                             [I CHOOSE THE CURSE?]
                             You were my ruin – ndingazange
                             ndakwenza nto imbi.
                             [THOUGH I DID NOTHING TO HARM YOU.]
                             You poisoned me with your deeds.
                             You are the shadow that fell on my life
                             and made a child of me through fear.
                             I have hated you so long and now...
                             YOU WANT TO LOOK INTO MY
                             HEART? SIES!

ELEKTRA and ORESTES circle KLYTEMNESTRA.
A WOMAN from the CHORUS begins UMNGQOKOLO
(Split-Tone Singing).

KLYTEMNESTRA: (*To herself.*)
                             [57]It comes upon me as prophesied.
                             I was the two-footed lioness that bore
                             these wanting wolves.
                             I killed – and now must die.
                             But not without a fight will the destroyer
                             be destroyed.
                             [58]BRING ME MY MAN-KILLING AXE!

---

57   Adapted from Cassandra in *Agamemnon* (SU) [1256, 1258]

58   Adapted from *The Libation Bearers* (SU) [1889]

*The CHORUS joins the UMNGQOKOLO (Split-Tone
Singing).*

*KLYTEMNESTRA is suddenly up and racing towards the
pick-axe lying on the ground. ORESTES and ELEKTRA
close in. ELEKTRA snatches the axe before she can reach it.
ORESTES grabs a flailing KLYTEMNESTRA, pulling her to
the ground. She cannot move.*

> (*Pleading.*)
> [59]My son, – hear me – For I will say this
> only once.
> Upon this breast you often lay asleep.
> And from here you sucked the milk that
> made you strong.
> I gave you life. And if you take mine –
> you will never know peace again.

ELEKTRA: (*Circling her mother and brother, axe in
hand.*)
This night's end is already written.
Our destiny must be played out!

KLYTEMNESTRA: Nothing...nothing is written.
Do not choose to be me. [60]The hounds
that avenge all murder will forever hunt
you down.

ELEKTRA: This is the son of Agammemnon.
His hour is come at last.

---

59   Adapted from *The Libation Bearers* (IJ), ll 1115–16 [896–8]

60   Adapted from *The Libation Bearers* (IJ), ll 1147–8 [924]

ORESTES: (*In rage and pain.*)
                    YOU HAVE MADE ME WHAT I AM!!

KLYTEMNESTRA: (*Lowering her head, ready for the blow
                    from the axe.*)
                    Then strike my child – and be done.

xviii: shift

*ORESTES lifts the axe high over his head, but as he prepares
to kill his mother, a **WOMAN** from the **CHORUS** starts to
sing a haunting song. **ORESTES** tries to shake off the sound
of it.*

ELEKTRA: Yini? [WHAT?] Why do you pause?

*He lifts the axe again, but the **WOMEN** rise and move across
the performance area. He tries several times to see the deed
through – but cannot.*

ORESTES: NeZinyanya ziyayazi lo nto…
                    [EVEN THE ANCESTORS KNOW THIS…]

Throwing down the axe.

                    I cannot shed more blood.

ELEKTRA: But the Furies demand it. They cry out
                    for more.

ORESTES: (*Grabbing her.*) There is still time, Sister.
                    Walk away.

Rewrite this ancient end.

ELEKTRA: (*Wrenching herself loose.*)
                  Don't ask me to forget my hatred! There
                  can be no forgiveness!
                  Slay her like the animal she is.

ORESTES: I am tired of hating.

ELEKTRA: Go then and keep company where you
                  belong…
                  Na bafazi! [WITH WOMEN!]
                  I will do this thing on my own.

ORESTES: WHAT IS IT YOU WANT?

ELEKTRA: (*She screams from her soul.*)
                  VENGEANCE!
                  An eye for an eye and a tooth for a tooth!

ORESTES: That was the curse of our Mother's House.
                  I have been there tonight and it's empty.
                  It's a circle with no end.

ELEKTRA: My father's blood will be paid back here
                  tonight.
                  I am from the House of Atreus. I will do
                  what must be done.

*She grabs the axe and runs at **KLYTEMNESTRA** screaming.*

xix: rises

*The **WOMEN** of the **CHORUS** move swiftly as one. They
grab **ELEKTRA** and overpower her.*
*__ELEKTRA__ screams in rage as they wrestle the axe from
her hands. They restrain her and she finally breaks down
and weeps for all the injustices done to her, her brother and
her father. She slowly finds her breath. UMASENGWANA
(Milking / Friction Drum) begins its deep, haunting sound.
__ELEKTRA__ emerges from the knot of **WOMEN**. She and
__ORESTES__ are focused on their mother – still cowering centre
stage. They crawl towards her slowly. KLYTEMNESTRA
– uncertain of what they will do to her – draws back in terror.
As they reach their mother, they slowly stand together and
extend their hands to help her up. Once on her feet, she is a
broken woman. She backs away and leaves the performance
platform, resuming her place at her Testimony Table.*
*The **WOMEN** of the **CHORUS** explode into song, circling
brother and sister. __ELEKTRA__ and __ORESTES__ embrace,
weeping. They have triumphed over their destiny of
vengeance.*
The cycle has been broken.
*The Diviner of the group steps forward. She prays, as the
others chant in response.*

> [61]Ndinqula aMambathane
> [I PRAISE THE MBATHANES]
> OoMatshaya, ooXesibe
> [I PRAISE THE MATSHAYAS, THE XESIBES]
> Ndinqula uBhomoyi [I PRAISE BHOMOYI]

---

61   The below praises are from Nofenishala Mvotyo. They include the names
of her Ancestors, as well as her prayer for South Africa. The content of this
praise / prayer varies at each performance.

USophitsho, uNgqolomsila

[SOPHITSHO, NGQOLOMSILA]

UYemyem [YEMYEM]

Ndinqula uGcaleka, uTshilo

[I PRAISE GCALEKA, TSHILO]

Mthi wembotyi [MTHI WEMBOTYI]

Nditsho kumama ke Xa nditshoyo...

[I'M TALKING TO MY MOTHER IN PARTICULAR,
WHEN I SAY THAT...]

Ndiqulela umanyano lwabantu

Abamhlophe nabantsundu

[I PRAY FOR UNITY BETWEEN BLACK AND WHITE]

Sinqulela abantwana bethu

[WE PRAY FOR OUR CHILDREN]

Bayeke ubundlobongela nokubulalana

[THAT THEY MAY STOP CRIME AND KILLING EACH
OTHER]

Sicela umsebenzi lo siwenzayo

[WE ASK THAT THE WORK THAT WE ARE DOING]

Siwenze ngempumelelo – sibenamandla

[MAY WE DO IT WITH SUCCESS – AND POWER]

Sithethe inyaniso.

[AND SPEAK THE TRUTH.]

epilogue

*The CHORUS, ELEKTRA and ORESTES stand facing the
audience.*
*KLYTEMNESTRA is at her Testimony Table. She speaks into
the microphone.*

KLYTEMNESTRA:	It falls softly the residue of revenge…
	Like rain.
	And we who made the sons and
	daughters of this land, servants in the
	halls of their forefathers…
	We know.
	We are still only here by grace alone.
	[62]Look now – dawn is coming.
	Great chains on the home are falling off.
	This house rises up.
	For too long it has lain in ash on the
	ground.

The full company stands in silence looking out at the audience.
A fine powdery substance gently floats down on them –

As lights fade to black.

---

62   Adapted from *The Libation Bearers* (IJ), l 1199 [961]

CPSIA information can be obtained
at www.ICGtesting.com
Printed in the USA
BVHW052112190123
656648BV00006B/68

9 781840 028553